EXCESS ALL AREAS

EXCESS ALL AREAS

A Lighthearted Look at the Demands and Idiosyncrasies of Rock Icons on Tour

SUE RICHMOND

ILLUSTRATIONS BY WILF HANSON

Backbeat
Books

An Imprint of
Hal Leonard Corporation

Published in 2014 by Backbeat Books
An Imprint of Hal Leonard Corporation
7777 West Bluemound Road
Milwaukee, WI 53213

Trade Book Division Editorial Offices
33 Plymouth St., Montclair, NJ 07042

Printed in the United States of America

Riders appear courtesy of Q magazine, used by permission.

Book design by Damien Castaneda
Illustrations by Wilf Hanson

Library of Congress Cataloging-in-Publication Data is available upon request.

ISBN 978-1-61713-596-5

www.backbeatbooks.com

To Wilf and Katy—my beautiful and
talented children and my inspiration

{3} MORE TEA, VICAR?

4 Bryan Adams
4 Ash
5 Black Sabbath
6 Cornershop
7 Eels
8 Elton John
10 Embrace
11 The Go! Team
12 Goldfrapp
13 Kasabian
14 Kiss
15 The Music
17 Ozzy Osbourne
18 Usher

{21} WE NEED OUR FIVE-A-DAY

22 Charlotte Church
23 Hear' Say
24 Hot Hot Heat
25 Ladysmith Black Mambazo
26 Lee "Scratch" Perry
27 Leftfield
28 Lordi
29 Moby
30 Public Enemy
31 The Rapture
32 Robbie Williams
33 Rollins Band

{35} NEW TOWELS PLEASE!

36 Badly Drawn Boy
37 Bloc Party
38 David Bowie
41 Bowling for Soup
42 Ian Brown
42 Culture Club/Boy George
44 DJ Shadow
45 Elbow
46 Hal
47 James
48 Jimmy Eat World
50 Juliette and the Licks
51 The Pogues
52 The Polyphonic Spree
53 Slipknot
54 Terrorvision

{57} CHAMPAGNE LOVERS!

58 B*Witched
58 James Brown
60 Busta Rhymes
61 The Charlatans
62 Chemical Brothers
63 Jamie Cullum
64 LCD Sound System
65 Lighthouse Family
66 Van Morrison
66 The Prodigy

{69} SMOKIN'

70 AC/DC
72 Ryan Adams
73 Basement Jaxx
74 Black Rebel Motorcycle Club
75 The Coral
76 Goldie Lookin Chain
77 Happy Mondays
78 Interpol
79 The Levellers
80 Motörhead/Lemmy
82 Ocean Colour Scene
83 Placebo
84 Rufus Wainwright
84 Amy Winehouse

{87} THE DRINKS ARE ON US

88 Audioweb
89 Corinne Bailey Rae
90 The Beatles
92 Def Leppard
93 Electric Soft Parade
94 Elvis
96 Eminem
98 Hard-Fi
99 Kaiser Chiefs
100 Mylo
101 Napalm Death
102 Beth Orton
103 Reef
104 Roots Manuva
105 Scissor Sisters
106 Stereophonics/ Kelli Jones
108 The Zutons

{111} YOU WANT WHAT?

112 Bloodhound Gang
113 Blur/Graham Coxon
114 Electric Six
115 Gay Dad
116 Gorillaz
116 Iggy Pop
118 Jurassic 5
118 The Killers
120 Lemon Jelly
121 Mogwai
122 Monster Magnet
122 Mötley Crüe'/Nikki Sixx
124 The Offspring
125 Orbital
126 Super Furry Animals
127 Westlife
128 Yo La Tengo

Introduction

Excess All Areas takes you on a roller-coaster backstage ride into the unpredictable and surreal world of the band contract rider. A *rider* is a shopping list of items, usually food and drink requested by the band, and forms part of the contract for the concert venue.

If you think Van Halen's eighties demands to remove all of the brown M&Ms from the sweet bowl in their dressing room was a tad precious, think again.

We delve into the dressing rooms of our favorite bands, from Black Sabbath to Usher, and have a good old rummage around, discovering a penchant for expensive champagne, enough towels to dry an army, the odd boa constrictor, inflatable sumo outfits, and soda water—just for spilling on the floor.

Rather surprisingly, it has been known for bands to refuse to go on stage if something is missing from their rider. So, if the request is for a specific jar of peanut butter, ice without square edges, water from the top of Mount Olympus and twelve pairs of white tube socks, you sure as hell need to get them, if only to avoid the wrath of a 10,000-strong audience.

The revelations in *Excess All Areas* will leave you stomping your feet and shouting for more.

skills needed to

EXCeSS ALL AreAS

*

BRYAN ADAMS

Green tea; fresh lemons; honey; unsalted raw almonds; biscuits; loaf of crusty white bread; two bottles of white wine; beer; colas; still water; kettle; teapot; coffee maker (with supplies); toaster.

....

ASH

72 large cans Stella Artois/Red Stripe/1664 strong lager; 12 cans Strongbow cider (if not proper alcoholic cider don't bother, we'll have more beer); 18 cans mixed soft drinks and 18 cans Diet Coke; 4 liters orange juice; 72 x 500 ml bottles of still water, ideally with sports tops or at least 6 with sports tops; 1 bottle of good white wine (no chardonnay); 3 bottles of Jack Daniel's/Jim Bean/Jameson's; 6 Red Bull energy drinks; unlimited supplies of tea, coffee, milk, sugar, cups, spoons etc., *plus* kettle or an urn. All drinks to be iced down with a good supply of cups and glasses and ice in an ice bucket. This is very important and the ice must be in the dressing room at least 1 hour before showtime. Crisps; fruit (including at least 6 bananas); sweets; chocolate; biscuits; full deli tray of meats and cheeses for 14 people; bread; rolls; butter; mustards; sauces; mayonnaise; knives; plates; etc.

....

*

BLACK SABBATH

1 small fresh fruit tray (skinned papaya, mangoes, blueberries, raspberries, strawberries, oranges, pineapples, etc.); 1 box of Carr's water biscuits; 4 fresh New York-style bagels; 1 small box of PG Tips tea bags; 1 box of Throat Coat tea bags; small portion of chips plus salsa and guacamole. Pita bread and hummus; 8 large bottles of Perrier; Soya Kaas hickory-smoked flavor soy cheese and cracker tray; 1 large carton Edensoy Milk, original flavor; 3 packets of instant hot chocolate; cloth napkins; 4 boxes of Kleenex; 4 bars of soap; 4 ice buckets with tongs.

❋

CORNERSHOP

1 bottle of quality vodka (properly chilled); cranberry juice; herbal tea; tea; honey bears (for squeezing into tea); Gatorade; mineral water; 5 bottles of Nantucket Nectar soft drink; 1 bottle of red wine; 1 bottle of white wine; 24 bottles of Budweiser; basket of pretzels; Pringles; Brie; baguettes; 2 boxes of Fruit Loops.

**"1 Furby stuffed toy;
1 Teletubby stuffed toy."**

EELS

Large tray fresh fruit; large tray of assorted clean vegetables; tray of assorted cheese (Gouda, cheddar, Brie, Swiss); deli tray assorted cold meats; selection of cereals; 1 loaf of wheat bread and 1 loaf of sourdough; 1 jar *organic* peanut butter; 1 jar *organic* strawberry or raspberry jelly; 1 box stone wheat crackers; 1 box sesame crackers; 1 bag *organic* tortilla chips; 1 large bag potato chips; 24 bottles still natural spring water (Evian preferred) at room temperature; 1 gallon fresh orange juice; 1 gallon cranberry juice; 6 cans Sprite, 7-Up, or Slice; 6 cans classic Coca-Cola; 6 bottles lemon/lime Gatorade; half gallon semi-skimmed milk; 2 liters plain, natural rice milk; 1lb of fresh ground Italian roast coffee; a clean and fully functional kettle; assorted herbal and English tea; 1 box sugar cubes; plates/cups/cutlery; 1 box napkins; 1 box unscented aloe tissues; 12 large white bath towels; selection of candles; small box matches; 2 bouquets of fresh cut flowers; 1 bottle opener; 1 Furby stuffed toy; 1 Teletubby stuffed toy. **No chocolate or candy should be in the Eels dressing room**.

ELTON JOHN

Six foot sofa; love seat; easy chairs; chairs; table lamps; floor standing lamps; coffee table; 6 food banquet tables (covered with white linen table cloths); large green plants; large arrangement of colored flowers (*no chrysanthemums, lilies, carnations, or daisies*). 4 large San Pellegrino bottled water or 12 small bottles; 4 large Evian or 18 small bottles of water; 8 Diet Coke (*must be in cans*); 4 Diet 7-Up/Diet Sprite; 1 pint of fresh squeezed orange juice; 1 pint of fresh 2% milk; 1 hot water kettle; 1 assortment of teas; coffee; sugar; uncut fresh lemons to include in English breakfast tea; Equal brand sweetener.

✳

EMBRACE

24 bottles of water (non-carbonated); 8 bottles of orange juice; 48 cans of lager (Carling Black Label or similar); 24 cans of Coca-Cola; 2 bottles of good quality red wine; 1 bottle of Jack Daniel's; selection of nuts and crisps; deli platter (sandwiches and fruit); plastic cups (enough); 1 large tub of ice. Available during soundcheck and load in: coffee (regular and decaffeinated); hot water; assorted teas and honey; 8 hot well-balanced meals (1 vegetarian) or cash buyout of at least £10 per person.

> **Selection of the day's English papers including music press. A toaster.**

✳

THE GO! TEAM

Breakfast buffet (bread, jam, cereals, etc.); sandwiches (including veggie and non-dairy); selection of salads, raw veg, and dips (for the healthies); selection of cheeses, meat, chocolates, etc. (for the rest); selection of breads; crackers; bowl of fruit; hot meal (with veggie option) for 15 people or buyout of £10 per head. Tea, black and green; 24 cans of premium lager; 24 bottles of local ale; 24 cans of soft drinks; 12 small bottles of natural fruit drink/smoothies; 1 bottle of vodka; 1 bottle of red wine; 1 bottle of white wine; 60 small bottles of water. At least 1 (preferably 2) lockable non-smoking dressing room(s) with a full-length dressing mirror, access to backstage toilets. Selection of the day's English papers including music press. A toaster.

❋
GOLDFRAPP

12 towels (clean if possible); 6 large bottles of still mineral water; 4 large bottles of sparkling mineral water; various fruit juices (to include cranberry/pineapple, etc.); a selection of herbal and non-herbal teas; fresh coffee; milk; selection of tea bags. Various snacks (crisps/tortilla chips/chocolate/sherbet dabs); selection of glittery false eyelashes (no blue ones); selection of jelly (not with fruit bits); and toffee ice cream. 1 whip (not PVC) or riding crop (leather handle); table tennis bat (wooden handle, stippled, Acme or better); 12 bottles of premium lager (chilled— not Kestrel); 4 bottles of quality dry white wine (French/Italian); 1 small bottle of quality vodka; 1 small bottle of Jack Daniel's. Hot meals for 16 people to include 2 vegetarian options; no cling film. Plates; cutlery; Branston pickle; etc.

> " Various snacks (crisps/tortilla chips/chocolate/sherbet dabs), selection of glittery false eyelashes (no blue ones), selection of jelly (not with fruit bits), and toffee ice cream. 1 whip (not PVC) or riding crop (leather handle), table tennis bat (wooden handle, stippled, Acme or better). "

✳

KASABIAN

3 multi packs of salt and vinegar square crisps; brown sugar; 80 PG Tips tea bags; 1 box of Pop Tarts. 4 liters of Smirnoff vodka; 12 cans of Red Bull; 1 bottle of absinthe; 2 pints of milk; 4 bottles of Jack Daniel's. 1 boom box; 6 tins of oxygen; 200 Marlboro Lights; 1 pair of nail clippers; 4 nail brushes; 4 black combs, no smaller than 6 inches long.

....

" 1 boom box; 6 tins of oxygen; 200 Marlboro Lights; 1 pair of nail clippers; 4 nail brushes; 4 black combs, no smaller than 6 inches long. "

KISS

10 freshly baked chicken/turkey breasts (5 of each); 1 fresh pasta (for 10 people) with sauce (marinara, Alfredo, and oil and garlic); 1 freshly imported Parmesan cheese with grater; 1 assorted fresh whole fruit basket for 10 people; 1 small chafing dish with freshly steamed corn (not on the cob and with butter on the side); 8oz tuna salad (no egg please); 1 loaf of rye bread with butter on the side; 1 small jar of Coleman's mustard; 1 small jar of Dijon mustard; 6 chocolate rice cakes; 6 caramel rice cakes; 1 small jar of black raspberry jam; 3 boxes of assorted crackers (including Wheat Thins); 2 cans of Pringles (BBQ and regular); 12 liters non-carbonated spring water; 1 liter of natural apple juice; 1 liter of fresh-squeezed orange juice; 2 half gallons non-fat and skimmed milk; 6 liter-sized bottles of red Gatorade; 12 pack each of Classic Coke, Diet Coke, and Pepsi; 12 pack Diet Sprite; 6 cans of Squirt; 6 bottles each of Lipton Ice Tea and Lipton Regular Ice Tea/lemon; 50 plastic Solo cups (16 oz); 1 hot water and coffee setup for 12; 1 small box Lipton tea; 1 pot of decaf coffee; 1 bottle of natural honey (8 oz); 8 whole unsliced lemons w/knife and cutting board; 30 packs of sugar, SweetN' Low, Equal, and Sugar in the Raw; 10 china dinner plates; 10 sets of cutlery; 1 8' table covered with tablecloth; 15 cloth table napkins; 10 large coffee mugs; 6 boxes of Kleenex tissues (the square Boutique boxes).

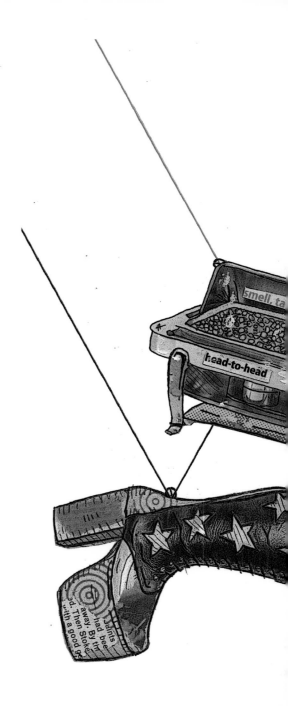

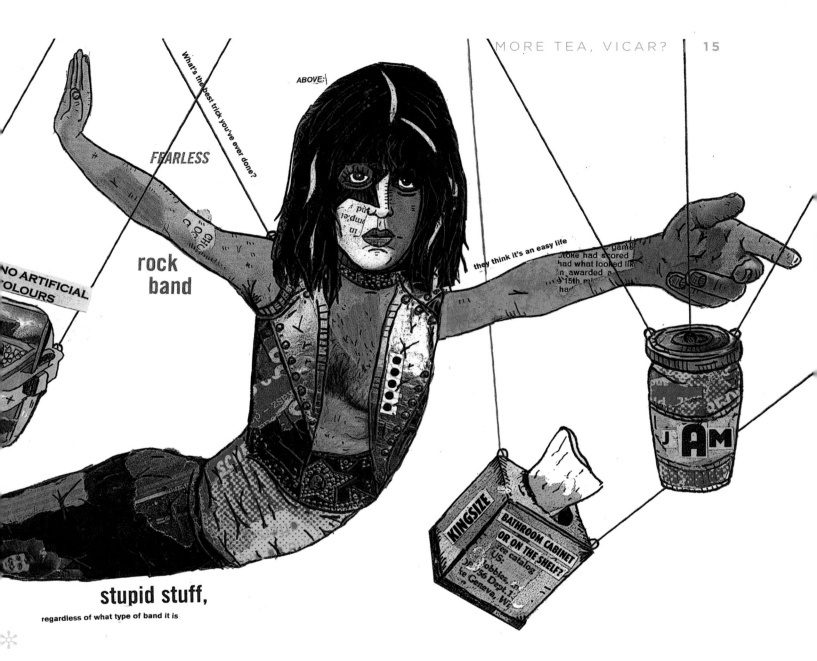

THE MUSIC

48 bottles of good quality lager; 2 bottles of good red wine; 36 small bottles of still water; a selection of sandwiches; a selection of fruit drinks; a selection of soft drinks (no diet); assorted crisps and snacks; assorted chocolate bars/ biscuits. Tea- and coffee-making facilities. 9 hot meals (2 vegetarian).

OZZY OSBOURNE

1 small fresh fruit tray (skinned and sliced papaya, mangoes, blueberries, raspberries, strawberries, oranges, pineapples, etc.); small fruit bowl with green apples, seedless green grapes, bananas; 1 box Carr's water biscuits; 4 fresh multigrain buns; 1 container fat-free cream cheese; 4 fresh New York-style bagels; 1 container fresh marinara sauce for dipping; 24 one-liter bottles Evian water; 4 liters spring water; 1 liter fresh-squeezed orange juice; 6 Diet Pepsis; 6 small bottles sparking water (Perrier or similar); 2 lemons with cutting board and knife; assorted herbal and Twinings black and Ceylon teas; 1 box Throat Coat tea; small carton non-fat milk; sugar; Canderel; honey; teaspoon; etc. Tea kettle or pot for boiling (no hot water in carafes); 3 sets of china and flatware; 3 large glasses; 3 large mugs; 12 16 oz clear Solo drinking cups; 1 bagel toaster; 1 box Kleenex; clean ice in ice bucket with tongs; paper napkins; 2 glass ashtrays. Mr. Osbourne's dinner of choice: boned, steamed fish—sea bass, orange roughy, or red snapper; no butter or oils!; baked potato; steamed veggies; pasta with marinara sauce (tomatoes and basil, *no meat*).

*

USHER

Non-fat yogurts; bagels, 10 servings of fruit; 6 oz of trout, tuna, cod, or white fish, grilled or baked; 1 cup of brown rice; 1 serving of vegetables; 1 chicken breast with yams (medium sized) and green salad with nonfat dressing; 20 protein bars, assorted flavors; selection of vegetables with low-fat dips; 10 cans of Diet Coke; cranberry juice; Evian water; hot water (Usher will bring his own Throat Coat tea from GNC stores).

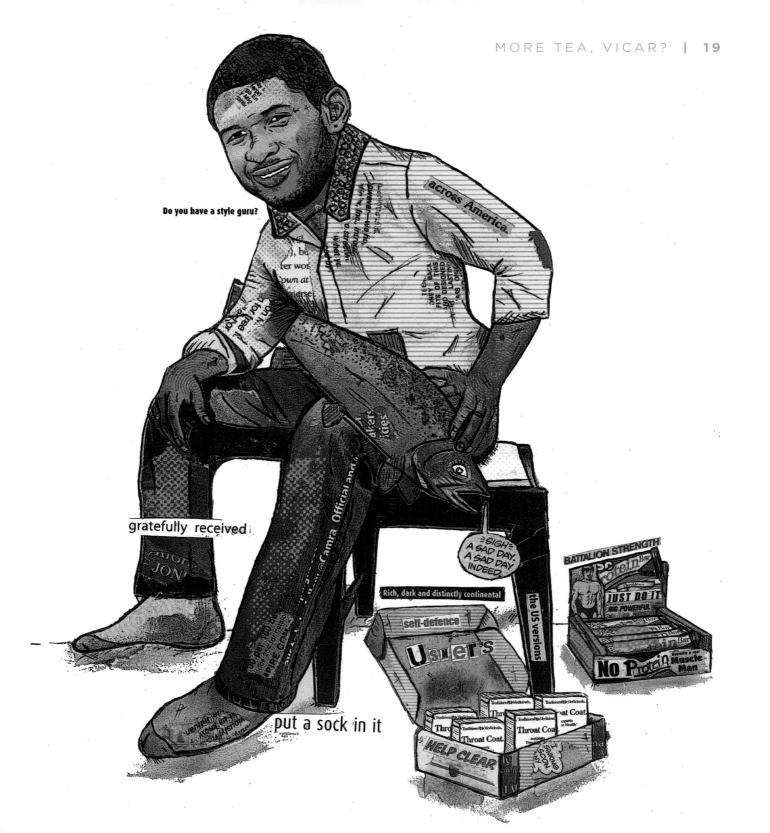

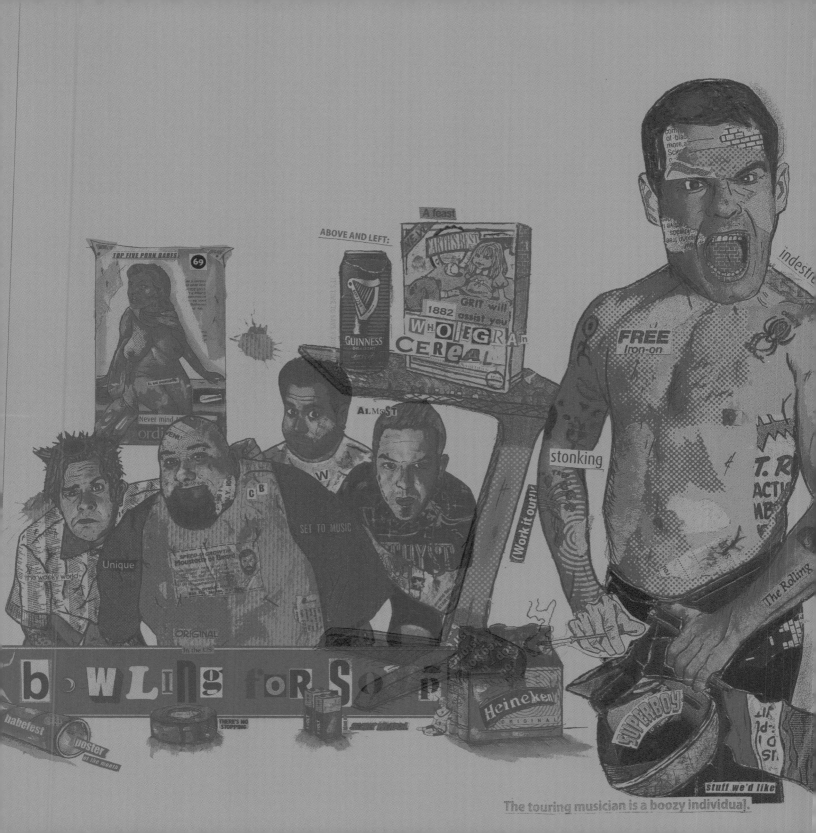

We Need Our Five-A-Day

CHARLOTTE CHURCH

1 crate of Diet Coke; 1 box of Evian water; Caesar salad; pieces of chicken, beef, and ham; steamed vegetables—asparagus, broccoli, carrots; lots of fruit—kiwi, strawberries, pineapple, and melon; pizza; bread—white and brown; English breakfast tea; coffee; milk; and sugar. Pasta—penne/spaghetti; plain rice; Maltesers; towels; iron and ironing boards.

HEAR'SAY

Deli tray—cheese, dips, crudities. Selection of sandwiches—including bacon and tuna. 1 bag Kettle chips—salsa flavor, fresh fruit (tropical if possible), Ginseng and berocca, royal jelly, 10 bottles of still water, crate of small bottles of water (25 in total), 24 bottles lager—preferably Japanese, 3 bottles white wine—New Zealand Cloudy Bay.

❋ HOT HOT HEAT

24 x 750 ml bottles non-carbonated mineral water, 12 x 12 oz cans of assorted soda drinks (Coke, 7-Up, Dr. Pepper, etc.), 8 cans Red Bull energy drink, hot coffee and tea with milk and sugar, refrigeration or enough ice to keep the above listed cold for the duration of the evening. Fresh whole fruit (apples, oranges, watermelon, grapes, etc.) and vegetables with dip. Assorted chips, pretzels, or a light snack. 1 x 8 oz can of Planter's brand cashew nuts. Wheat or sourdough bread, cheeses, crisp lettuce, cucumber, salt and pepper, French's yellow mustard, mayonnaise, etc. Sufficient cutlery, cups, plates, napkins, condiments, etc. for 6 people. 1 pint of hummus and pita bread. 36 domestic microbrews or imported beer such as Heineken or Stella Artois (or the equivalent in drink tickets), 1 flask-sized bottle of Jägermeister, 1 flask-sized bottle of bourbon, 6 pair of black tube socks. Hot, nutritious good quality meals with drinks and desserts (not fast food or pizza) for 7 people. If a hot meal is not possible, then a buyout of £10 (or equivalent in Euros) per person for seven (7) people shall be paid to the band's tour manager.

* LADYSMITH BLACK MAMBAZO

For 10 people—bottles of Pepsi; tea and coffee, with lots of sugar sachets; 10 cartons orange juice; five cartons pineapple juice (organic); cans of assorted fizzy flavored drinks; chicken breasts spiced (go heavy on the spice); maize (fresh); rice (fried with vegetables); assortment cooked vegetables; 10 mangoes; bananas; lychees (fresh not canned); breadsticks (spicy); pretzels; assorted cakes: chocolate, banana, ginger; 1 large bar fruit & nut chocolate.

LEE "SCRATCH" PERRY

Fresh fruit (must include bananas), fruit juices—various, still water—2 bottles, bottle of champagne, candles, incense, cookies (preferably large chocolate chip).

*

LEFTFIELD

Drinks on ice: 4 liters Coca-Cola (Classic Coke); 2 liters fresh orange juice; 1 liter each: cranberry, fresh apple juice, and mixed "exotic" fruit juice; 1 liter carbonated mineral water; 12 assorted soft drinks (Snapple, Gatorade, Tango, 7-UP, isotonic drinks, etc.); 48 bottles premium bottled lager (Budvar or Stella Artois); 2 bottles quality white wine (Chablis, chardonnay). Drinks not on ice: 1 bottle Jack Daniel's, 12 liters still mineral water (Volvic, Evian, or Spa) and 12 small bottles for stage use. 1 large assorted, washed whole fruit bowl for six (orange, apple, banana, melon, mango); 1 large bowl assortment of chocolate and mixed candy (use your imagination here!); 1 medium bowl assorted packed snacks, potato crisps, corn chips. 1 large ice bucket, replenished as required, 4 misc. English newspapers (as up to date as possible). Sufficient plastic drinking "glasses" (large and small), thermal cups, 1 box of super-soft tissues, napkins, bottle opener, 4 ashtrays, matches, rolling papers, and grass please.

....

"1 large ice bucket, replenished as required, 4 misc. English newspapers (as up to date as possible). Sufficient plastic drinking 'glasses' (large and small), thermal cups, 1 box of super-soft tissues, napkins, bottle opener, 4 ashtrays, matches, rolling papers, and grass please."

LORDI

Peanuts, fresh fruit, other light snacks, still water, various soft drinks (very important to have a few cans of Dr. Pepper and Pepsi Max), coffee, milk, tea (not herbal). Drinking straws, clean towels.

*

MOBY

2 cases of good quality beer (48 bottles); 6 bottles Bud Lite; 2 bottles of good quality red wine (Merlot, Cabernet Sauvignon, or Shiraz); 10 bottles of rehydrating soft drink (e.g., Gatorade); 4 cartons of organic fruit juice, including orange; 3 cases of 33 ml still water; 1 small cheese plate including Gruyère, Havarti, cheddar. A selection of organic fresh fruit, to include bananas, grapes, apples, oranges, and strawberries; a selection of organic vegetables and salads, including avocados, spinach, carrots. 2 loaves French bread; large bag of organic tortilla chips; organic salsa medium; organic cereal (raisin bran, muesli); 3 x 1 liter/quart cartons of organic soya milk; 1 carton fresh semi-skimmed milk; selection of teas, including English breakfast, herbal, and decaffeinated, with honey and sugar; selection of candy bars; use of a blender for juices and smoothies; 12 Emergen-C multivitamin sachets or equivalent.

> **"**No pork, no alcoholic beverages.**"**

*

PUBLIC ENEMY

Note: All food must be kosher or halal. 3 gallons of Poland spring water; 6 large bottles of Evian water; 1 bucket (mixed) Kentucky Fried Chicken; 10 fresh baked fish (snapper or whiting); 9 gallons various juices, in cans or cartons (pineapple, apple, orange, grape, grapefruit). 2 large cheese pizzas; 1 large tray with various cheeses; 1 x 6 pack of Dr. Pepper; 1 x 6 pack Pepsi; family size packs of cookies (Sunshine Hydrox, chocolate chip, and vanilla fingers); fresh fruit: Washington apples, oranges, grapes, pineapples, and three bunches of bananas; 1 large party tray of cold cuts: kosher meat, turkey, lettuce, tomatoes, American and Swiss cheese, roast beef. Steamed vegetables: broccoli, corn, string beans, mashed potatoes. All trays should have plastic covers. Tea, coffee, honey, lemon, sugar, hot cups, spoons, cream, and milk. **No pork, no alcoholic beverages.**

✳

THE RAPTURE

Lunch and dinner for 14 people (or USD $20.00 equivalent buyout), 3 cases of bottled beer (Corona, Becks, Heineken), 24 bottles of still spring water, 6 bottles premium quality dry cider, 1 bottle of whisky, 1 bottle of dry white wine, 1 case of mixed soft drinks (Coca-Cola, Sprite, Diet Coke), 6 cans of ginger ale, 1 liter of orange juice, ample hot and cold cups. All drinks should be iced down and kept ice cold. 1 plate of assorted fresh fruits and vegetables, 1 packet of pistachio nuts, 1 packet plain M&Ms, cheese plate and crackers, 12 clean hand towels, 4 white bathrobes, 2 packs of 20 Marlboro Lights or Camel Lights cigarettes. 1 used paperback novel (English language please).

> "1 used paperback novel (English language please)."

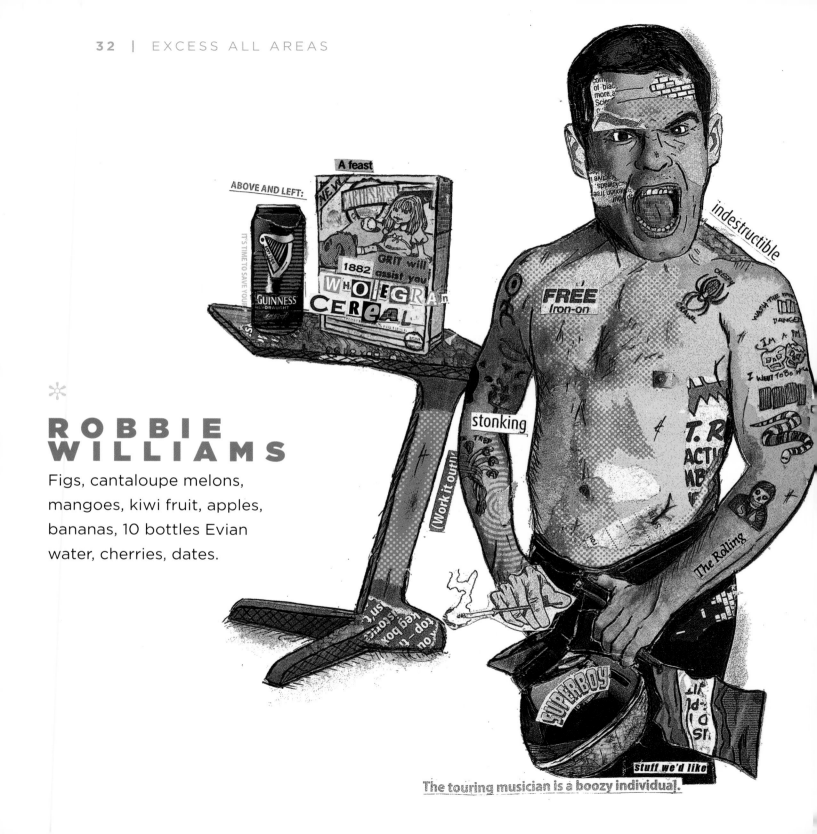

ABOVE AND LEFT:

ROBBIE WILLIAMS

Figs, cantaloupe melons, mangoes, kiwi fruit, apples, bananas, 10 bottles Evian water, cherries, dates.

The touring musician is a boozy individual.

*

ROLLINS BAND

Coffee pot with "fresh" real dark roast Italian coffee and real milk; 36 bottles of still water (*no Evian*); tuna or deli platter with good fresh food—real cheese, lettuce and tomato, etc.; 2 loaves of fresh bread with condiments for making sandwiches; 2 large boxes of cereal (wholegrain) with 2 liters of milk and 2 liters of soy milk; 2 dozen assorted bagels and pastries; 2 tubs of cream cheese or spreads; 2 liters of fresh assorted fruit juices; 12 protein bars, chocolate and assorted flavors. 1 tray of assorted fresh fruit, 12 bottles of mineral water with gas, 2 large bags of tortilla chips and 2 jars or tubs medium salsa, 3 tubs of hummus, 12 bottles of local beer and 6 cans/bottles Draught Guinness (*no Heineken*), 6 cans Coca-Cola and 6 cans Coke Light.

"Coffee pot with 'fresh' real dark roast Italian coffee and real milk; 36 bottles of still water (*no Evian*); tuna or deli platter with good fresh food— real cheese."

NeW ToWELS PlEaSE!

BADLY DRAWN BOY

48 cans or bottles of good quality lager (Budvar, Stella, Beck's), 2 bottles of good quality red wine, 6 cans of Draught Guinness (to come with pint glass), 1 bottle of Jack Daniel's, 2 liters of Coca-Cola (not Pepsi), 1 liter of lemonade, 24 small bottles of *still* mineral water (that's *still* mineral water), 1 liter of grapefruit juice, 1 liter of orange juice, glasses, plastic cups and *ice*, kettle with tea, milk, coffee, sugar, selection of chocolate and fruit, 20 Marlboro Lights, 15 clean towels (paper *not* acceptable).

BLOC PARTY

Sandwiches (inc. vegetarian), snacks, Jaffa Cakes, Tunnock's Tea Cakes, Sainsbury's Caramel Wafers. Tea and coffee should be made available on arrival of crew and should remain available all day. 1 lemon; 2 limes; 1 small jar of honey; organic fruit bowl: apples, seedless grapes, bananas, satsumas, strawberries; 2 loaves of bread (1 white, 1 wholegrain); 1 box of Weetabix/Oat Cluster cereal; 2 large bars of chocolate (Cadbury's); dried apricots; butter/spread; selection of cream cheese; cheddar; hummus; peanut butter; Marmite; mayonnaise; guacamole. Quality cold meats, pâté, smoked mackerel, salmon. 12 live yogurts; salad items: tomatoes, lettuce, cucumber, fresh broccoli, baby carrots. Dips and snacks, e.g.: crisps, nuts, Doritos, Mini Cheddars. Good quality hot meals for 14 persons (including 4 veggie). 36 bottles of good quality lager (no Stella Artois, no cans), 8 cans of Draught Guinness, 4 cans of cider (Stowell Press, organic), 2 large bottles of vodka (preferably Absolut, 1 flavored), 1 bottle of quality white wine, 1 x 2 liter bottles of lemonade (R. White's, Schweppes), 12 cans of Coke, 6 cans of Diet Coke, 2 cartons of orange juice, 2 liters of semi-skimmed milk, 12 cans of Red Bull, assorted canned soft drinks, 1 case of bottled still water, 1 bottle of quality red wine, tea/coffee/herbal teas. 30 fresh towels, use of kettle and toaster, 1 tube of Berocca (or similar), cutlery, plates, bowls, mugs, and glasses.

*

DAVID BOWIE

12 cup Mr. Coffee machine; 6 coffee mugs—china; fruit bowl for 3 people—apples, oranges, mangoes, etc.; fresh orange juice; 9 large Evian; supply of boiling hot water; honey; lemons and cutting board with knife; make up mirror with good lighting; full length mirror; rolling clothes rack; 12 towels; 2 boxes of tissues; 110 v power supply; outside phone line.

**"1 roll duct tape (grey),
2 x 9 volt batteries. "**

*

BOWLING FOR SOUP

15 clean towels, 2 cases cold bottled water, 2 coolers or very large bins of ice, 24 plastic cups, 12 Diet Cokes and 12 Cokes, orange juice, cranberry juice, 2 rolls paper towels, 2 loaves bread (1 white, 1 wheat), lots of sandwich meat, several cheeses, biscuits, salad, dill pickles, Tabasco or some other hot sauce, 2 cases (24 cans each) Budweiser or Heineken (no Stella please), 1 case of Super Strongbow, 1 large bottle Absolut vodka, 1 large bottle Jack Daniel's, 1 bottle white wine (sauvignon blanc), 1 bottle red wine (merlot), 1 roll duct tape (grey), 2 x 9 volt batteries.

IAN BROWN

2 bottles champagne; 24 assorted beers; 24 small bottles still mineral water; 24 hand-sized towels; isotonic drinks; Coca-Cola, Sprite, etc.; selection fruit juice; 1 carton Benson and Hedges or Rothmans cigarettes; large selection fresh fruit "which must include bananas, ripe and ready to eat"; hot chicken meal for 12 people including some vegetarian options; "no pork dishes (pig)."

CULTURE CLUB

Selection of fresh fruit for 10 people—Culture Club and backing musicians, selection of fresh vegetables and dips (hummus, taramasalata), 20 liters of Evian water (non-carbonated), 6 liters of Perrier water (carbonated), a lot of ice, cups and glasses, tea spoons, a kettle for boiling water, a selection of teas to include Throat Coat and Earl Grey, fresh ground Colombian coffee, sugar, honey, cinnamon sticks, a liter of full-fat milk, a liter of semi-skimmed milk and liter of soy milk, 2 cases (48 bottles) of Beck's lager, 4 liters of fresh squeezed orange juice, 24 cans Coca-Cola, 20 cans Diet Coca-Cola, 60 towels "of the bath size."

✳

DJ SHADOW

Fresh fruit for 10 people, selection of sandwiches (25 percent vegetarian), cheese, cold meats (white and red), crudities, crackers, crisps. Energy and chocolate bars; cereals (gluten-free if possible); 10 hot meals with fish, chicken, and vegetarian options, or take out equivalent to £15 each, including a list of local restaurants: Asian, Thai, and Japanese. 2 cases good quality beer, 48 cans of assorted soft drinks, 2 liters each fizzy and still mineral water, 2 liters low-fat milk, 2 liters each of cranberry and orange juice, selection of herbal and fruit teas and coffee, lemons and honey, ginseng capsules, list of all local record shops, 30 towels.

> " Ginseng capsules, list of all local record shops, 30 towels. "

"All wholesome, non-polluting, non-GM, organic-type stuff, wherever possible, please). Soap, 18 towels, local tourist information and city guide."

✳

ELBOW

36 bottles of water (preferably Volvic), 72 bottles of good quality imported beer (Budvar, Beck's), 2 bottles of red wine, 1 liter bottle of vodka, 2 liters tonic water, 6 cans of Red Bull, 1 liter Coke, milk. Crisps, wholesome veggie soup, bananas and apples, 1 packet of muesli. Hot evening meal for 17 people (4 vegetarian) (all wholesome, non-polluting, non-GM, organic-type stuff, wherever possible, please). Soap, 18 towels, local tourist information and city guide.

> **"1 life-size Frank Carson cardboard cut-out."**

HAL

48 cans/bottles of Guinness; 12 cans/bottles of quality imported lager, preference is Red Stripe (please, no Stella Artois); 2 bottles of Jameson Irish Whiskey; 2 cases (20 bottles per case) of still bottled water in 50 cl bottles; 1 carton of fresh orange juice; 1 carton of fresh cranberry juice; 1 bottle of tonic water; assorted fruit juices and smoothies; tea and coffee. Fresh root ginger, jar of honey, 1 pack of Marlboro Lights, selection of cheeses and meats, assorted bread and rolls with butter and knives, chips and dips, fruit bowl. Dinner for all band and crew (8 people). Please note that vegetarian options will be required (no meat, no fish), as well as meat and fish dishes. A buyout of 20 euros per person is always preferable. Selection of sandwiches, pizzas or the local takeaway delicacy for aftershow. 30 good quality large towels; 2 large trash/rubbish/refuse containers; 10 dark, nearly new hand towels. 1 life-size Frank Carson cardboard cut-out.

*

JAMES

2 bottles vintage champagne (chilled); 1 bottle single malt whisky (if not, then Jameson); 1 bottle gin; 1 bottle Vladivar vodka; 1 bottle good dry white wine (Chablis/Sancerre); 2 bottles good quality red wine; 48 bottles Carlsberg; 12 large bottles non-gas mineral water; 6 bottles Slimline tonic water; 2 liters strong cider; selection of fresh vegetables with juicer; 12 bottles health drinks (e.g. Rocket Juice/Grainaissance/Odwalla); large bowl fresh fruit; selection of fish, chicken, and vegetarian sandwiches; selection of chocolates; plenty of plastic cups; metal cutlery; waste bins, etc. Tea-making facilities with Bamboo cereal beverages, posters and promo material of the event, selection of South Park videos for the entertainment lounge, 15 bath towels, 6 hand towels, and 3 tablets of fresh soap.

"Selection of South Park videos for the entertainment lounge."

*

JIMMY EAT WORLD

1 bottle Maker's Mark whisky, 2 bottles of Pellegrino or soda water, ice and plastic cups, 2 cases beer: Sierra Nevada or Red Stripe, pita bread and hummus, crisps and salsa, 1 case assorted soft drinks (no Pepsi), assorted herbal tea and Throat Coat tea, 2 lemons, honey, pot of coffee, hot water for tea, 2 large bottles cranberry juice, 1 large orange juice, 1 deli plate with cold cuts and cheese, 1 fresh fruit and vegetable plate, 3 cases bottled water, 12 bottles of Gatorade or similar sports drink, tube of Tums heartburn and acid indigestion tablets, 1 bottle good white wine, 1 bottle good red wine, 1 box of Emergen-C or Berocca, 24 hand towels.

*
JULIETTE AND THE LICKS

Honey, sweetener, 1 box of breakfast cereal (Bran Flakes, muesli, etc.), 2 loaves of bread, a selection of meats and cheeses, peanut butter and jam, margarine/butter, 3 cans of tuna, mayonnaise, chocolate snacks, hot meals for eight people. Coffee, Throat Coat tea, 1 liter of soya milk, 2 liters of semi-skimmed milk, orange juice, various sodas (Coke, Diet Coke, Sprite, etc.), 24 bottles of continental beer, 1 bottle of Scotch/Irish whiskey, 48 small bottles of still water, kettle and cups, 12 clean small white towels, 8 clean large white towels.

*

THE POGUES

24 bottles of beer, 1 bottle of gin, 1 bottle of vodka, 1 bottle of dry white wine (Soave or Frascati), 1 bottle of Martini, 1 bottle of brandy, 1 bottle of champagne, 1 bottle of ginger beer, 2 bottles of Coke, 2 bottles of sparkling water, 2 bottles of still water, 1 bottle of iced tea, 1 bottle of rock shandy, 2 bottles of non-alcoholic Beck's. A selection of fish, vegetarian, and pasta dishes; chocolate; packets of Marlboros, Marlboro Lights, and Benson & Hedges (Carrolls in Dublin); 48 large, clean towels.

> **"Enough ice to take a bath in."**

THE POLYPHONIC SPREE

Facilities to make tea, coffee, hot chocolate in the hall. A selection of sandwiches and rolls for 30 people. 1 large pizza, no cheese please; 2 large vegetarian pizzas. 12 one-liter bottles of spring water (no Evian please); 24 small plastic bottles of still spring water, room temperature, not chilled please; 12 pack Coke; 12 pack Dr. Pepper; 12 pack Diet Coke; 24 bottles of Budweiser; 48 x 440 ml cans of Stella Artois; 24 x 440 ml cans of Heineken; 8 x 440 ml Smith's/Caffrey's beer; 2 x 770 ml bottles of Jägermeister; 1 bottle Jack Daniel's; 6 bottles good quality red wine; 10 Red Bulls; assortment of fresh fruit; assortment of crisps; nachos; chips; peanuts; assortment of sweets; 4 pints of chocolate milk; 2 pints of milk; kettle with an assortment of tea bags, coffee, sugar, etc.; enough cups and glasses for the above. Enough ice to take a bath in, 30 bath-size towels, one box of good quality washing powder (non-biological).

❋

SLIPKNOT

6 dozen towels for Slipknot only! 5 assorted scented candles and incense, 12 cooked boneless and skinless chicken breasts, 12 pack of Ultra Slimfast rich chocolate protein drinks on ice, 4 boxes of assorted Celestial Seasonings teas, 1 container of clean ice, 2 half gallons of 1 per cent milk on ice, 10 assorted pudding packs ready to eat, half gallon of 100 percent pure grape juice on ice, 10 assorted Gatorades on ice, 10 packs of assorted gum, 1 four pack banana chocolate chip muffins, 1 box Kudos peanut butter bars, 1 half gallon chocolate milk, 6 cans of Chef Boyardee ravioli, 1 large bag of assorted Starburst fruit chews, 6 assorted cans of Campbell's chunky soup, box of baby wipes, 12 pairs of white tube socks.

....

"6 cans of Chef Boyardee ravioli, 1 large bag of assorted Starburst fruit chews, 6 assorted cans of Campbell's chunky soup, box of baby wipes, 12 pairs of white tube socks."

✳

TERRORVISION

1 bottle Moët & Chandon champagne ("No Moët, no show-ey, no Chandon, no band-on"), 1 bottle tequila, 1 liter bottle Famous Grouse, 2 liter bottles Smirnoff vodka (red) or Absolut (blue), 6 liter bottles Italian/French dry white wine, 24 bottles Corona/Sol (on ice), 24 Stella Artois (on ice), 4 Red Bull/Lucozade energy drink (on ice), 4 7-Up (on ice), 4 liter bottles Schweppes Bitter Lemon, 12 liter bottles Evian/Volvic still mineral water, 24 cans Coca-Cola Classic, 1 liter Schweppes tonic water, 4 liters fresh orange juice, 1 deli tray, 1 cheese tray, 24 Kit-Kats (must have foil wrappers), salad and dressings, brown and white bread and butter, assorted fresh fruit (must include bunches of grapes), assorted crisps/chips/peanuts. Fun-sized chocolate bars, 20 half-liter plastic glasses, 20 liter plastic glasses, corkscrew/bottle opener/plenty of ice. Full-length mirror, 20 brand new clean towels ("the kind that don't dry you but leave fluff all over you").

"20 brand new clean towels ('the kind that don't dry you but leave fluff all over you')."

CHAMPaGne LOVErs!

❊
B*WITCHED

12 bottles Evian water; assorted raw vegetables—carrots, cucumber, celery, peppers, cauliflower; 10 chicken and mayonnaise sandwiches on white; honey and lemon with hot water (for the voice); big bowl of assorted nuts; basket of mini Cadbury's chocolates; tin of Chupa-Chups; 20 Crunchies; orange juice; tea. For after the show: 2 packets of Philadelphia cheese and crackers, 1 case of champagne.

❊
JAMES BROWN

Hooded hair dryer, iron, ironing board, towels, soap, deli tray with assorted meats and cheeses, coffee, tea, soft drinks (Coke products), Gatorade, champagne (Cristal or Dom), 1 electric golf cart.

" 1 electric golf cart. "

*

BUSTA RHYMES

24 bottles of apple juice, 1 box low-fat soy or rice milk (vanilla or plain, no carob), herbal teas, 1 case of beer (Budweiser), 1 fifth of Courvoisier, 1 case of Guinness stout, 6 bottles of Cristal or Moët & Chandon champagne, 1 bottle of red wine, 1 fresh fruit tray, peanut butter and assorted jellies, assorted breakfast cereals (Rice Krispies, Frosted Flakes), assorted munchies (candy and crisps), 2 boxes of Lifestyles and Rough Riders condoms. NB: There is to be no beef or pork in the food or vicinity of Busta Rhymes's dressing or catering room.

✳

THE CHARLATANS

15 hot three-course meals (fast food, e.g. McDonald's, pizza, etc. will not be acceptable). If it is not possible to provide meals, a cash substitute will be required to the value of £25 per head. 2 bottles vodka (Smirnoff, Absolut), 1 liter; 2 large bottles cognac (Rémy Martin); 2 large bottles Jack Daniel's; 6 bottles white wine (pinot grigio); 6 bottles champagne (Bollinger); 2 cases Stella Artois imported; 2 cases Hoegaarden or similar white beer; 1 case Evian mineral water, 1 liter bottles; 2 liters tonic water; 1 case sparkling mineral water; 1 case assorted soft drinks, including Coke and Diet Coke; 2 liters orange juice; 2 liters cranberry juice; 2 liters grapefruit juice; 60 Silk Cut; 20 Marlboro Lights. A selection of crispy vegetables/salad tray with assorted dips, cheeses, biscuits; savoury selection to include sandwiches, crisps, and nuts. Fresh fruit, chocolate bars. 2 Montecristo cigars for the manager!

✳

THE CHEMICAL BROTHERS

1 crate Perrier Jouët champagne, 2 bottles Dom Pérignon champagne (preferably 1963), 1 case quality white wine (preferably Chablis), 1 case quality red wine (preferably Rioja), 1 bottle Stolichnaya vodka (preferably Black Label), 2 bottles Maker's Mark bourbon, 1 bottle Islay single malt whisky, 4 cases Wroclaw Polish lager, 4 cases Querétaro Mexican beer, 2 bottles Tanzanian rice wine, Golden Wonder prawn cocktail crisps, assorted sandwiches, many choccy biccies, cheese, nuts.

✳

JAMIE CULLUM

Marks & Spencer sandwiches, crisps, nuts, yogurt. Fruit—bananas, apples, grapes, pineapple, etc. Definitely pineapple. Honey and lemon (not too big), hot lunches for 7 people after soundcheck or £20 per head. 12 small bottles of still mineral water, 1 bottle of good quality red wine, 1 bottle of good quality white wine, 20 bottles of good quality lager/beer, 4 cans of Guinness, 1 half bottle of Myers's rum, 20 bottles of Moët & Chandon, 6 cans of Coke, various fruit juices, small bottle of worcester sauce. Kettle, tea, coffee (fresh ground please), milk, sugar, cups and spoons, bottle opener, and knife. Ice, but not square, must have no straight edges; cups; plates; cutlery; bottle opener; and napkins. 1 full-length mirror (must have lights round it), 6 towels, tables, chairs, and 1 deckchair.

✻

LCD SOUNDSYSTEM

Sandwiches for 10 (1 vegetarian option), crisps, nuts, biscuits, cheeses, fresh fruit (minimum of 10 pieces), fresh-cut vegetables. A good quality two-course hot meal (no fast food) for 10 people. Of these meals, 2 to be vegetarian (no meat, fish acceptable). Assorted chocolates, cookies, 1 loaf of white bread, a jar of peanut butter and a jar of jam (important!), other sandwiches for 10 people, to include vegetarian selections. Water, fruit juices, tea and quality, dark-roast coffee (espresso or Italian roast preferred), 1 bottle of Jameson Irish Whiskey or Maker's Mark bourbon, 3 bottles of quality champagne, 24 small bottles of quality lager, 1 four pack of Draught Guinness in cans, 1 six-pack of local microbrew, 4 x 16 oz bottles of Gatorade (normal flavors please), 1 large carton of fresh orange juice, 48 x 12 oz bottles of still mineral water, 12 liters of sparkling water, 10 Oranginas, 6 cans of ginger ale or ginger beer, 1 x 36 packet box of Emergen-C drink mix (tangerine), 12 cans of assorted soft drinks (non-diet). "Hot Toddy" ingredients: honey, lemons, cinnamon sticks, cloves, fresh ginger. 15 clean towels, sufficient cutlery, cups, plates, napkins, etc. Note: please use non-disposable silverware, plates, cups, and napkins, where possible. Likewise, no styrofoam.

LIGHTHOUSE FAMILY

1 bottle Cordon Rouge champagne, 1 bottle Stolichnaya vodka, 1 bottle Jack Daniel's, 1 case of beer Grolsch/Beck's, 6 cans Draught Guinness, 6 cans Draught Bitter, half a case of Coca-Cola, 4 liters orange juice, 1 liter apple juice, 1 liter pineapple juice, 1 bottle good red wine, 1 bottle French dry white wine, 1 case 500 ml bottles still water, 1 packet cotton buds, for removal of make-up ("we do have female backing singers"), tea and coffee to include herbal teas, clear honey, lemons, etc. Fruit bowls/cakes/biscuits/chocs and nuts ("for each dressing room"), 1 case small bottles water, 2 liters mango juice ("for drinking on stage").

VAN MORRISON

1 liter mineral water (still); 1 liter orange juice; 1 liter apple, cranberry, or grapefruit juice; 2 or 3 low-fat fruit yogurts; fresh fruit bowl; cold buffet for two people (should include salad, cold chicken, cheese, and ham); assorted biscuits and cake; English breakfast tea; filter coffee machine with regular and decaf coffee; milk; honey and fresh lemon; 1 box of tissues. 2 hand towels, 4 bottles vintage white wine, 4 bottles Chablis Premier Cru white wine, 4 bottles top-quality red wine, 4 bottles Dom Pérignon champagne, 1 bottle Hennessy cognac.

THE PRODIGY

A packet of Crunchy Nut cornflakes, six bowls, six spoons, and a bottle of Dom Pérignon champagne.

"Cartons of cigarettes and tobacco so (singer) Brian Johnson can roll his own."

A C / D C

Tea, coffee, sparkling water, Coca-Cola, Sprite, Gatorade, 1 bottle white wine, 1 bottle red wine, Bailey's (for drummer Phil Rudd), cheese, raw vegetables, sweets, chewing gum. Proper meal with, for example: salad, mashed potatoes with gravy, sausages or lamb cutlets or beef, custard and cake. Cartons of cigarettes and tobacco so (singer) Brian Johnson can roll his own.

*"*1 copy of the *New York Times*, 1 copy of the *New Yorker*, 1 working AM radio with CD player—if CD facility unavailable, then just an AM radio is fine.*"*

*

RYAN ADAMS

2 packs of Marlboro Lights (plus matches), 1 pack of Camel Lights, 1 pack Natural American Spirit cigarettes, 1 tray of assorted sliced fruit, 1 tray of assorted sliced vegetables, 1 tray of assorted cheese, Boursin (for guitarist Bucky Baxter), 1 bottle of carrot juice, herbal tea, coffee, 1 six-pack of Heineken, 2 bottles of Sterling red wine, 2 wine glasses, 1 bottle of Stolichnaya vodka, 1 pint of Myers's rum, 2 bottles of tonic water, plenty of bottled water, 4 limes, 8 clean towels, 2 ashtrays, Big Red chewing gum, 1 copy of the *New York Times*, 1 copy of the *New Yorker*, 1 working AM radio with CD player—if CD facility unavailable, then just an AM radio is fine.

BASEMENT JAXX

1 tray of cold meats; 1 tray of cheese, hummus, and non-meat sandwich fillings; a selection of fresh bread rolls (minimum 25); 2 sliced loaves; butter/margarine/mayonnaise; 4 liters of orange juice; 4 liters of apple juice; 4 liters of cranberry juice; fresh tea/coffee/milk; honey/lemons; fresh fruit bowl; 12 cans of Red Bull; 20 liters of mineral water; 12 cans of Diet Coke; 12 cans of Coke/Tango; 2 bottles of red wine; 2 bottles of white wine; ice; 2 packs of rolling papers; 40 Marlboro Lights; 60 bottles of quality lager; 1 bottle Jack Daniel's; 1 bottle of vodka; knives/forks/spoons/plates/cups—glasses must be supplied for the above.

BLACK REBEL MOTORCYCLE CLUB

6 bottles of Jack Daniel's, 6 packets of Marlboro Lights, 3 packets of Camel Lights, 2 crates of Stella Artois, 1 crate of Red Stripe, assorted chocolate bars and crisps, 1 bottle of red wine, assorted selection of sandwiches, 1 tray of fresh fruit.

*

THE CORAL

48 bottles of Budweiser or Rolling Rock Beer (iced), 1 bottle of vodka (Absolut), 1 bottle tequila, 1 bottle good red wine, 60 x small bottles of still mineral water (non-sparkling), 24 cans of Coke (no Diet), 24 assorted cans of Sprite, Dr. Pepper, etc. (no Diet), 4 liters fresh orange juice, apple juice, pineapple juice, and mango juice. 2 bunches of bananas and some apples and some oranges, fresh root ginger, fresh lemons, honey, 1 large fridge or large bucket full of ice (all day) for beer. 1 corkscrew, tin and bottle opener, 80 Marlboro Lights, 6 Rizla king-size slim papers, an endless supply of ice. 24 packets of crisps (McCoy's, Monster Munch, Seabrook's), 4 different packets of milk chocolate biscuits, 2 large white loaves (thick), 4 large tins of Heinz baked beans, 1 x 250 g Anchor spreadable butter, 8 pairs of black socks, 8 cotton T-shirts, no sandwiches, 2 pizzas (to arrive at 8 p.m.): 1 margherita and 1 meat feast. Catering for 18 people.

> ❝ 1 ounce of
> top-quality
> skunk weed,
> 2 sexy DVDs. ❞

GOLDIE LOOKIN CHAIN

Nuts and crisps, fresh fruit, tray of cheese, hummus and other non-meat sandwiches, deli tray (meat), tea/coffee (not instant), 6 cans of Red Bull, 12 assorted sodas (Irn Bru, lemonade, ginger beer, etc.) 2 bottles of red wine, 60 bottles of Beck's, 1 bottle of Jack Daniel's, 2 liter bottle of cognac. 8 packets of King Size silver/blue Rizla, 40 Marlboro Lights, 40 Silk Cut, 40 Benson & Hedges. 1 ounce of top-quality skunk weed, 2 sexy DVDs.

HAPPY MONDAYS

Tea and coffee facilities with kettle; honey and lemon; assorted soft drinks: Coke, Diet Coke, lemonade, etc.; assorted fruit juices: orange, cranberry, pineapple, etc.; 2 cases of still mineral water; 3 cases of large cans Stella Artois (brewed in Belgium, not UK); 1 bottle Bushmills whiskey; 2 bottles of Absolut vodka; 1 bottle Courvoisier brandy; 2 bottles of quality red wine (New World); 2 bottles of quality white wine (New World); 2 bottles of Yates's Australian Original Wine (suitable for Blobs); 60 Marlboro Lights; 60 Benson & Hedges; 20 Camel Lights; 20 Silk Cut Ultras; 100 Juve Ultras; 6 packs green king size Rizlas; substantial cold buffet to include sandwiches, pies (Holland's), quiches, crisps, dips, nuts, chocolate, etc. (some vegetarian); cups; ice; plates; etc. After show (on no account must this be placed in the dressing room before the show): 1 bottle of absinthe.

> "After show (on no account must this be placed in the dressing room before the show): 1 bottle of absinthe."

INTERPOL

2 fifths of Ketel One vodka, 2 fifths of Jameson's, 1 fifth of Sauza Silver tequila, 48 bottles of Stella Artois, 24 bottles of Corona, 1 bottle of red wine, 12 cans of Coke, 1 box of Emergen-C powdered vitamin drink (even days orange, odd days tropical), 1 gallon fresh orange juice. Bunch of celery, 3 packs of Tofurky, 3 packs of fake salami, assorted fresh vegetables (no cauliflower), sliced turkey, sliced honey ham, good quality dark chocolate candy bar, large pizzas (not Domino's), small Dijon mustard, pack of Camel Lights, pack of Camel Filters, pack of Red Gauloises, copies of *The New York Times*.

THE LEVELLERS

Hot coffee; fresh milk; and hot water for making tea; teabags including English breakfast, Earl Grey, and herbal. 1 liter soya milk, 4 chocolate bars, 10 cans various soft drinks and 10 cans of Coca-Cola, 4 Lucozade or isotonic sports drinks, 20 liters spring water, 5 liters fizzy water, 2 liters orange juice, 1 liter grapefruit juice, 1 liter apple juice, 2 bottles quality red wine, 2 cases good quality lager, 2 liters Absolut vodka or tequila or malt whiskey, 2 packs Camel Light cigarettes, 2 packs Golden Virginia tobacco, 4 packs blue Rizla cigarette papers, 4 boxes matches, 2 English newspapers—not *The Sun*.

*

MOTÖRHEAD

1 bottle Jack Daniel's; 1 bottle Jim Beam; 1 bottle vodka; half case
Carlsberg Special Brew; 3 cases Miller/Amstel Light/San Miguel; 1 case
strong dry apple cider; 1 case still bottled water; 1 bottle Perrier; 1 case
Coca-Cola; half case Pepsi Cola; 6 bottles lemon and lime Gatorade; 4
liters fresh orange juice; 4 liters fresh milk; 5 packets Reese's Peanut
Butter Cups; 3 bags assorted crisps; 1 bowl assorted fruit and nuts; 2
packs Marlboro Red; 2 packs Benson and Hedges; a deli tray, featuring
assorted cheeses, meats, pickles, etc.; assorted breads (including brown)
and crackers; butter; salt; pepper; mustard. A constantly refreshed
supply of ice cubes.

❋ OCEAN COLOUR SCENE

48 cans lager, 24 cans cider ("for making snakebite"), 1 bottle white wine, 1 bottle red wine, 1 bottle dark rum, 1 bottle gin, cans of Coke, bottles of tonic water, selection soft drinks ("for the ladies"), bowl of fruit, selection of chocolates ("for throwing about"), 1 pot of honey ("for Simon's throat"), 40 cigs x 4 (Gauloises for Damon Minchella, B & H Special Filter for Steven Cradock), Rizlas.

*

PLACEBO

Fresh brewed coffee/tea, milk and sugar, Throat Coat (slippery elm bark tea), 2 liters of 100% fresh unsweetened orange juice, 2 liters of cranberry juice, 2 liters of fresh apple juice, 2 liters of fresh grapefruit juice, 2 large bottles Schweppes Indian tonic water, 6 cans of Coca-Cola, 6 cans of Diet Coca-Cola, 48 bottles of quality lager (Beck's/Corona/Sol), 24 cans of Red Bull or similar energy style drink, 3 bottles of good quality red wine (Bordeaux, Chianti, Rioja), 6 bottles of good quality white wine (St. Emilion, Burgundy), 2 large bottles of Absolut vodka, 2 bottles of Moët & Chandon champagne, 1 bottle Campari, 1 bottle soda water, 3 cases (24 per case) of small (never large) bottled still mineral water. A small selection of snacks and assorted potato chips/nuts/candy/chocolate and a small selection of fresh fruit to include bananas, oranges, lemons, and root ginger. 1 small bottle (of squeeze-style) honey, 1 small packet of wet wipes, 1 box tissues, 3 packs Marlboro Light cigarettes, 1 pack lubricated condoms, 1 large tube Berocca.

RUFUS WAINWRIGHT

Fresh ground French roast coffee and filters with clean coffee maker, 36 x 2 liter bottles of still water (no Evian!), 6 Fresh Samantha or Odwalla organic juices, 1 box Capri Sun Fruit Punch drinks, 1 case bottled beer (local brews OK), 6 bottles O'Doul's or Sharp's non-alcoholic beer, variety soft drinks in single serving sizes on ice or in refrigerator. 2 bottles of red wine—Bordeaux, Médoc preferred. (Please give to tour manager directly, do not place this item in dressing room. Thanks.) 4 non-fat fruit flavored yogurts (Stonyfield, Columbo, or Danone), 1 pan of brownies, chocolate bars: dark and milk chocolate. Assorted tortilla chips and hot salsa; bowl of fresh, uncut fruit; small cut veggie platter with sour cream and chives dip; 1 jar of peanut butter; 1 jar of grape jam; 1 loaf of fresh bread; 2 packs Marlboro Red cigarettes and a lighter.

AMY WINEHOUSE

Absolut vodka (must be Absolut), Jack Daniel's, selection of fine beers (for the band), PG Tips teabags, water. Jerk chicken, rice and peas, pizza (margherita), vegetarian and non-vegetarian sandwiches, Doritos, nuts and bananas. Camel Lights, joss sticks (variety of fragrances), fresh towels, sign for the door that reads: "Only Big Boys Can Enter."

"Sign for the door that reads: 'Only Big Boys Can Enter.'"

WARNING
THIS COUPON IS WORTH £4
Just plug in
unique niche for herself
VODKA
pain
and struggle."
alcohol
SMIRNOFF
BIG
BOY'S onLy...
REGD.

Loveable pop kids

The DrInKS aRe ON US

at makes those four characters so rich?

AUDIOWEB

A selection of breads and rolls (granary/wholemeal/white); 2 packets of mature cheddar cheese; Golden Churn butter; a selection of sandwiches (vegetarian/meat and fish); assorted chocolate/nuts/crisps and snacks; a selection of cold soft drinks/water: Fanta, Lilt, Coke, etc. Fruit bowl to include Gwa Gwa tea and coffee; a good quality, substantial hot meal for nine people, one of which should be good quality vegetarian food. Fast foods such as McDonald's, pizza, etc. are not acceptable. The meal should be made up of a minimum of two courses with beverage included and should be based on but not limited to chicken, fish, pasta, etc. 48 large cans good quality lager, 6 cans of Murphy's Irish Stout, 1 bottle of good quality red wine, 1 bottle of vodka, 1 bottle of whisky (Johnnie Walker), 16 small bottles of mineral water, 2 large bottles Diet Coke, 2 large bottles of Coke, 4 liters orange juice, 4 liters cranberry juice, 4 liters grapefruit juice, 4 packets Silk Cut cigarettes. NB: If in-house catering cannot be provided, the management agrees to provide a buyout for the artistes of £10 a person.

*

CORINNE BAILEY RAE

3 large bottles of still mineral water at room temperature. No Dasani (Coca-Cola water) please! Selection of potato chips; a jar of Manuka honey; assortment of chocolates; 2 cases of Beck's beer; 2 bottles of Californian red wine—Merlot or Pinot Noir; 1 bottle of Absolut vodka; a selection of fresh cold cuts, cheeses, and sliced bread rolls for 14 people; 1 loaf of whole wheat bread; 1 stick of butter.

THE
BEATLES

A black and white
television set and a few
Coca-Colas.

> **"All leftover food to be donated to food center for homeless."**

DEF LEPPARD

Thai food—no meat, Chinese food—no meat. Shepherd's pie, 3 x 6-pack Budweiser, 2 x 4-pack Guinness (draught), 2 x 6-pack lite beer, 36 liter bottles Evian, 48 cans Heineken, 6 bottles non-alcoholic beer, 2 bottles Kendall Jackson Chardonnay, 12 cans 7-Up, 1 quart milk, 10 quart bottles Gatorade, half-gallon cranberry juice (Ocean Spray), 6 Pepsi, 1 liter soya milk, 1 bottle whiskey, 1 bottle Pouilly Fuissé white wine, 1 jar salsa, 1 large bag Doritos, peanut butter, honey. All leftover food to be donated to food center for homeless.

※

ELECTRIC SOFT PARADE

1 tube of Berocca; 48 large cans quality lager (Red Stripe, Stella, 1664, etc.; local lager is fine); 6 Strongbow; 6 Red Bull; 24 cans Coke; 12 cans Diet Coke; 3 liters orange juice; 1 liter cranberry juice; 48 500 ml bottles of still water; 1 bottle good white wine; 1 bottle of vodka; 1 bottle of Jack Daniel's/Jim Beam; unlimited supplies of tea, coffee, milk, sugar, cups, spoons, etc., plus kettle or an urn. All drinks to be iced down with a good supply of cups and glasses, ice for drinking in separate bucket. Crisps, plenty of fruit, sweets, and chocolate bars. Full deli tray of meats and cheese, bread, rolls, butter, condiments, plates, etc. Hot food—dinner for 11 people between 6:00–8.00 p.m., must consist of good quality hot food with a meat dish and a vegetarian alternative. Vegetarian soup to start and a pudding should be served in venue. (Alternatively, a buyout of £10 a person. Please arrange in advance if you wish to take us to a restaurant.)

*

ELVIS

10 soft drinks and 4 cups of water.

> **"A selection of Taco Bell (Mexican-themed fast food)— imported from America."**

EMINEM

2 bottles of Bacardi, 2 bottles of Hennessy cognac, 4 bottles of still mineral water, 2 cases of Mountain Dew (caffeine-charged soft drink)— imported from America, 4 bottles of orange juice, trays of assorted fruit. A selection of Taco Bell (Mexican-themed fast food)—imported from America.

HARD-FI

48 bottles mineral water; 24 cans good quality 5-percent-plus lager (e.g., Stella); 24 bottles Corona; 1 bottle quality white wine; 1 bottle quality red wine; 1 bottle quality vodka; 12 cans of Red Bull; 12 cans of Coke; 1 liter orange juice; a big box of munchies (chocolate, crisps, nuts, etc.); 1 box of PG Tips; 1 white loaf; 1 brown loaf; 1 meat/cheese deli tray with mustards, HP sauce, etc.; 2 large bowls of fruit; 6 limes. 2 couches, 1 refrigerator, 1 kettle, 1 toaster, 10 mugs, 20 plastic cups, 8 medium towels, 2 bags of ice.

KAISER CHIEFS

Tea and coffee-making facilities and a selection of herbal teas; 48 x 500 ml bottles of water (must be spring/mineral); 4 cans of assorted soft drinks (Sprite/Fanta); 2 liters of assorted fruit juices (not from concentrate), including freshly squeezed orange juice; 12 cans of 7-Up; 12 bottles of Budvar or Kronenbourg (no Stella, Grolsch, Beck's, or Budweiser); 6 cans of Carlsberg lager; 12 cans Red Stripe lager; 1 bottle medium white wine—Chardonnay or similar; 1 bottle of quality dark rum; 6 cans of regular Coke; 6 cans of caffeine-free Coke. 2 loaves of granary bread, 12 granary bread rolls, 4 French sticks, 1 tub of Flora (dairy-free), 4 pots of hummus, mayonnaise, a selection of sandwich meats/fillings, medium cheddar cheese (without color), salad including tomatoes and carrots. A fruit selection, including 10 bananas, apples, grapes, and oranges. A selection of crisps, nuts, biscuits, and chocolate. 11 good quality, freshly prepared hot meals. Please note that two of these are to be vegetarian and one is to be non-dairy. 2 limes, 1 bottle opener/corkscrew, 13A power sockets, low-level lighting in dressing room, rubbish bins, ashtrays, 1 full-length mirror, lots of pint and half-pint glasses/plastic glasses, mugs, plates and cutlery, 1 large bucket of ice, 20 medium-sized towels, 10 clean hand towels, 1 tube of effervescent Berocca.

✳

MYLO

1 bottle of single malt whisky, 1 bottle of French red wine, 200 bottles of lager, ice (in cubes), 4 bottles of Evian, 1 bottle of Sprite, 1 bottle of Sunny Delight. Hot vegetarian noodles, goat's cheese, baguette, bowl of fruit, rocks buns, monosodium glutamate, bottle opener (must be novelty), crayons (assorted colors), paper (135 gsm), folded map of the world, magazines (*Max Power*, *Razzle*, *Good Housekeeping*, etc.), *Descartes' Meditations*, cassette of rave music.

....

"Crayons (assorted colors), paper (135 gsm), folded map of the world."

*

NAPALM DEATH

1 fridge in working order; 80 cans or 40 liters of lager—Krombacher, Beck's, Löwenbräu, Carlsberg; 10 cans or 5 liters of Guinness or Murphy's; 46 cans of Coca-Cola and other soft drinks; 46 bottles of good-quality red wine; 3 liters of fresh orange juice; 12 cans of Red Bull or equivalent; 1 liter of Jack Daniel's; 1 bottle of spirits to be decided on the day by tour manager; 25 liters of still mineral water, Volvic or Evian. 10 small clean towels for use on stage; sufficient clean glasses, cutlery, and napkins.

❉

BETH ORTON

2 bottles of good quality wine (one white, one red); 24 cans of good quality local beer; 1 bottle of vodka (Absolut); 2 large bottles of Schweppes tonic water; 2 large bottles orange juice; 1 large bottle cranberry juice; 1 large bottle grapefruit juice; 30 assorted soft drinks (to include, but not limited to, diet/lite options); 6 bottles/cans "sports" drinks; 1 deli tray for 10 people—hummus, rice crackers, corn chips, etc.; olives, tomatoes, pita bread, feta cheese, avocados, sliced cucumbers, jar brown mustard (for Beth). Sufficient tea (including herbal), coffee, milk, lemon, sugar, ice, cutlery, etc., for 10 people to be available throughout the day. A good quality hot meal for 10 people approved by and at a time designated by the tour manager. Please be aware that Beth's meal must be wheat-free and gluten-free (e.g. chicken/fish/plain rice). In addition to this, five meals must be vegetarian. No junk food (i.e. McDonald's, etc.). If in-house catering cannot be provided, the management agrees to provide a buyout for the artistes of £10 per person.

REEF

Selection of bread and cheese, 48 bottles good quality beer, 2 liters orange juice, 1 bottle Spanish red wine, 1 bottle French white wine, 1 bottle whisky, 24 cans soft drinks, 16 bottles mineral water, various fruit (bananas, apples, oranges, kiwi fruit), various chocolate bars, various chips and Doritos, Ginseng health tablets or vials, 4 magazines (local music, skate, and surf fanzines), 4 stamped local postcards, 1 box Wet Ones moist hand wipes and soap, facilities to make tea: cups, kettle. 24 towels, 4 pairs socks (8–12 UK size), lemons, honey and sugar, 1 liter fresh milk.

ROOTS MANUVA

96 small bottles of still mineral water, 8 cartons of fruit juice, tea, fruit tea, coffee, 1 bottle of Moët & Chandon, 72 bottles of San Miguel, 12 cans of Guinness, 1 bottle of Courvoisier/Rémy Martin brandy, 1 bottle of Jack Daniel's, 1 bottle of Smirnoff Blue, 1 bottle good red wine. A deli tray of assorted cheeses and meats (no pork/pig products please), miscellaneous dips, 2 bags of tortilla chips, 14 hot balanced meals (5 vegetarian options, plus 1 nut-free). Dressing room to be kept at a reasonable temperature. 12 large clean towels, a fully working refrigerator, and/or a large supply of ice.

*

SCISSOR SISTERS

15 x 1 liter (or more) bottles of water for dressing room, 1 hot meal for 8 people (2 are vegetarian, the rest will eat anything), vegetarian deli tray, banana and sugar sandwiches on white bread, corn on the cob with extra butter, 1 bottle Grey Goose vodka (preferred) or Stoli if not available, 3 x 1 liter bottles tonic water, 12 cans Coke, 6 cans Diet Coke, 12 cans ginger ale (diet preferred). Hot water and herbal tea, ice, 1 bottle honey, 6 lemons, 18 clean towels, 6 Coney Island Whitefish. Jellybeans.

STEREOPHONICS

48 small bottles of still water, 1 liter orange juice, 1 liter cranberry juice, 1 liter apple juice, 8 cans Red Bull, 1 large bottle of tonic water, 1 bottle of good quality vodka (Stolichnaya/Absolut), 1 bottle of Jack Daniel's, 1 bottle of good single malt whisky, 2 bottles of good quality red wine (Barolo), 2 bottles of good quality white wine (Sancerre), 1 bottle of Jose Cuervo premium gold label tequila, 1 bottle of port (Taylor's vintage—pre-1970), 1 bottle of gin, 24 large cans of Stella lager, 24 bottles of Corona lager, 12 cans of Guinness, 12 cans of Boddingtons, 1 bottle lime cordial. 1 deli platter, to include cold meats and cheese selection, 4 fried chickens and some dry white toast, 1 large whole cucumber (NB not sliced), 12 large organic carrots, 8 lb box of Lion's Midget Gems, 8 Starbars, 1 bottle of HP sauce. 1 ass-shaped piñata filled with Cuban cigars and dark chocolate Cacique rum liqueurs, 1 box of indoor fireworks, 1 roll of black gaffer tape, 1 copy of *MCN* (Wednesdays), 1 copy of *South Wales Echo*, 1 copy of *El Gráfico*, 1 football and football strip of host city, 1 pack of Agent Provocateur playing cards, 1 DVD from this selection: *Twin Town, Zulu, Goodfellas, Alfie* (Michael Caine original), *Wild Geese, Where Eagles Dare, Enter the Dragon, Cool Hand Luke, Deep Throat.* 5 packets of Marlboro Lights, 2 tubes Berocca effervescent multivitamin tablets, 12 extra-large prophylactics, 1 local strippergram, 1 hedge trimmer.

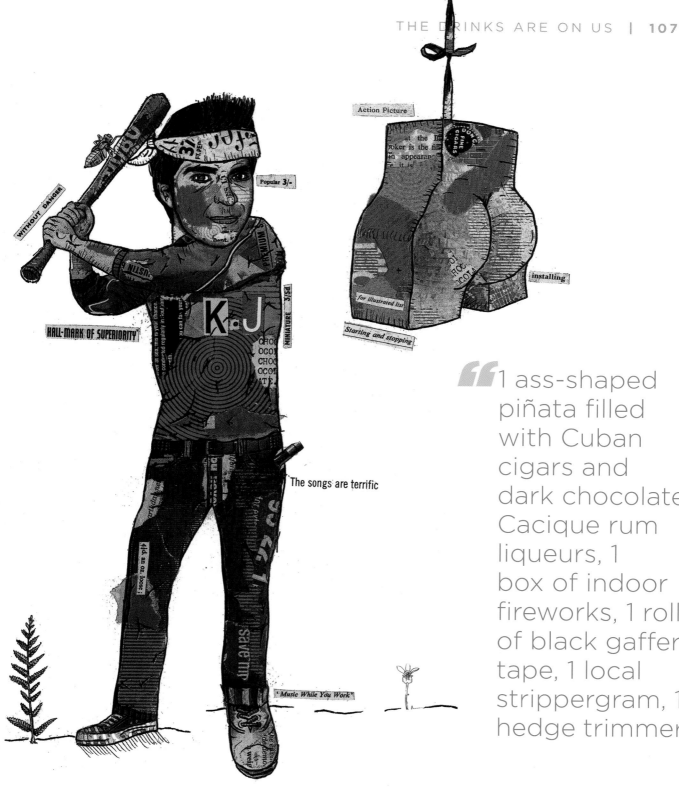

"1 ass-shaped piñata filled with Cuban cigars and dark chocolate Cacique rum liqueurs, 1 box of indoor fireworks, 1 roll of black gaffer tape, 1 local strippergram, 1 hedge trimmer."

THE ZUTONS

1 lemon, 1 large piece of ginger, a pot of honey, 24 assorted freshly made vegetable and meat baguette sandwiches. 1 bottle of Jack Daniel's, 1 bottle of vodka, 48 cans of lager (Stella Artois, Kronenbourg, etc.), 4 bottles of red wine (preferably Rioja, Shiraz, Cabernet Sauvignon, Merlot), 96 small bottles of still mineral water, 1 case of assorted soft drinks, 1 liter of apple juice, 1 liter of cranberry juice, 1 liter of orange juice, 1 liter of milk, coffee, tea and herbal teas, 2 cases of bottled beer (Kronenbourg, Beck's, Grolsch, etc.). 20 hand towels for stage use, 10 bath towels, flask to keep water hot, kettle, knife and chopping board, plastic glasses for drinks, and 6 wine glasses. Corkscrew. Plasma screens in their dressing rooms so that they don't miss their favorite team, Liverpool, in action.

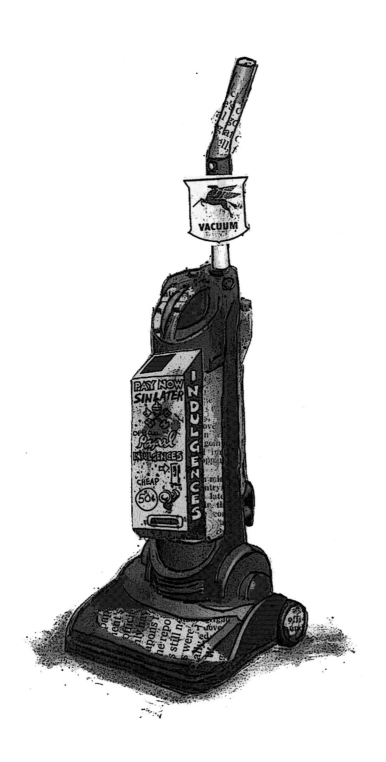

" Plasma screens in their dressing rooms so that they don't miss their favorite team, Liverpool, in action. "

YOU WANT WHAT?

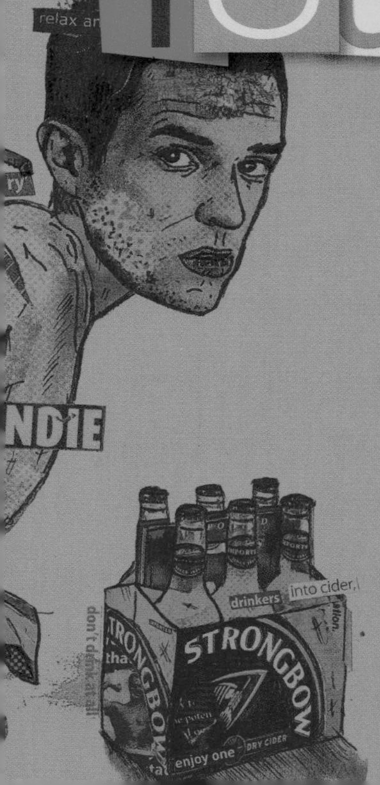

"1 fridge magnet of local interest."

BLOODHOUND GANG

Deli tray including: 1 uncut onion and 1 uncut tomato, 1 sharp knife for the above, deli mustard, low-fat mayonnaise, butter, salt and pepper; 1 giant size bag of low-fat Lay's potato chips; 1 bag of pretzels; 1 jar containing 6 hot dogs (frankfurters); fruit basket; half a gallon of Tropicana orange juice; half a gallon of Ocean Spray (Cran-Raspberry); half a gallon of grapefruit juice; 1 case (24 cans) Coca-Cola; 1 case (24 cans) of mixed Mountain Dew, Dr. Pepper, and Sprite; 1 case (24 cans) Dr. Pepper (to remain in case for use in show); 1 case of Red Bull; 2 gallons of freshly brewed iced tea; 4 cases of non-carbonated, non-mineral water in plastic bottles (for stage); 4 cases of cold Samuel Adams, Newcastle Brown, Beck's, or Rolling Rock beer; 2 six packs of Coors Lite; 2 liters of Absolut vodka; 1 liter of Jägermeister; 1 bottle of Tawny Port wine (from Oporto, Portugal); 1 bottle of quality red wine; selection of candy bars, Oreo cookies, Snickers, Twix, etc. 1 large packet of Skittles, separated by color (bassist is obsessive compulsive), several assorted packs of gum and breath mints, 3 cigars, 1 small rhesus monkey skeleton, 1 bottle Pert 2-in-1 shampoo/conditioner, 1 bar Coast/Dove soap, 1 copy *USA Today*, 4 packs of Marlboro Red or Prince of Denmark cigarettes, 2 packs of Parliament Lights or Camel Lights, 1 tin Kodiak Wintergreen chewing tobacco, 1 fridge magnet of local interest.

*
GRAHAM COXON/ BLUR

Double Deckers, Welsh cakes, 5 lbs scrag end (or metric equivalent), bucket of hot water, tea and coffee (fresh, not instant), scrumpy with bits, local lagers, Middlin' wine. Ornamental rockery, old tin bath, hoof knives (inscribed with venue name), soap, towels, toothpicks, Derby County Subbuteo team, spare undergarments (selection of sizes), false facial hair.

> **Spare undergarments (selection of sizes), false facial hair.**

ELECTRIC SIX

4 cases of quality lager, 3 carton of orange juice, 20 small bottles of water, 6 cans Red Bull, 2 bottles of Jack Daniel's, 2 bottles of vodka, 2 bottles of red wine (Spanish Rioja, preferably 1998 or earlier vintage), selection of soft drinks including Cola (preferably 50 percent Pepsi/50 percent Coca-Cola), hummus and pita bread selection (or other "healthy" deli-tray type option), mixed sandwiches for 11 people, bowl of fruit (bananas are essential), peanuts, crisps, etc., 12 pre-washed clean towels, 1 .38 special, 6 rounds .38 ammunition.

> **"A bigger dressing room, repainted to remove graffiti, stickers, and band branding; padded doors that can't be slammed noisily."**

*

GAY DAD

A bigger dressing room, repainted to remove graffiti, stickers, and band branding; padded doors that can't be slammed noisily; a Le Corbusier chaise longue (original pony skin); coded door entry for bouncer; a decent sized mirror; en-suite bathroom; and, where possible, a steam shower for band. 24 bottles of Leffe (Belgian Love Beer), one case of Badoit: the very best mineral water, Elderflower cordial, two bottles of Taittinger or Pommery to mix, Rollmop Herring, vine tomatoes (preferably Moroccan; the Provençale variety are rather demode), a selection of cheeses, bread, and olive oil. The latest edition of *Honcho* magazine.

> **"Two Goth girls must also be installed, dressed in Michelle Pfeiffer's Catwoman outfit."**

✳

GORILLAZ

Noodle—a Dreamcast set up with a copy of Resident Evil: Code Name Veronica. She'd also like a Buddhist shrine, with candles and incense already lit. 2D—a box of Bueno bars and some bottles of Yop and his photograph of Adam Yauch placed above Noodle's Buddhist shrine. Russell—a buffet of burgers and two box-fresh corduroy Vans, size 4. Murdoc—dressing room floor must be covered with cat litter so he can scratch around and mark his territory. Two Goth girls must also be installed, dressed in Michelle Pfeiffer's Catwoman outfit. Murdoc must also have an ample supply of asparagus wrapped in beef to make his breath and piss really honk.

....

✳

IGGY POP

Seven dwarves, pizzas to give to the homeless, a copy of the *New York Times*, and pre-chopped broccoli florets, to make them easier to throw away!

....

"Seven dwarves."

JURASSIC 5

Water (from the top of Mount Olympus), towels (woven from the wool of a sheep sheared on the day of the gig), a selection of fruit (handpicked by virgins), ginger beer, strawberry M&Ms, earplugs (preferably previously worn by members of Oingo Boingo), six crack whores.

THE KILLERS

12 pack Coca-Cola (from USA), 6 bottles Snapple Iced Tea, 8 bottles Strongbow cider, 2 cases Evian spring water, 24 bottles Coors Light, 12 bottles Beck's beer, 2 bottles red wine (Shiraz, Merlot), 1 liter Maker's Mark, 1 liter Absolut vodka, 12 cans Red Bull. Sainsbury's hummus (important), pepperoni pizza, 1 loaf sliced bread, 1 jar Jif peanut butter, 1 jar strawberry jam, assorted candy bars x 6, 1 pack of Jaffa Cakes, assorted deli meats, cheese for sandwiches, fruit bowl, Spanish rice. Personal masseuses. Large plastic cups/bowls (no styrofoam). 1 national newspaper.

*

LEMON JELLY

6 bottles of Evian, 2 liter bottles of San Pellegrino mineral water, 1 bottle of Stolichnaya, 1 bottle of Chablis, 12 bottles of Stella Artois, 4 bottles of local micro-brewery beer, 1 large vegetable platter (celery, cucumber, carrots, tomatoes, etc.), 2 mixed sushi platters, 1 fresh fruit bowl, 1 small loaf of wholemeal brown bread. Sandwich makings to include: cheeses, beef, tomatoes, alfalfa sprouts, assorted nuts and snacks (no chocolate). 1 box of Love Hearts, 1 box of Black Jacks, 1 box of Fruit Salads, 1 box of Jelly Babies, 1 Darth Maul costume.

"1 painting by a gifted child or local amateur."

MOGWAI

No Nestlé products, please. Sandwiches for 16 people (half vegetarian), hummus, salad, and pita bread. Tea including fruit teas, 48 bottles/ cans of good quality lager beer (no American beer, no Stella Artois), 3 bottles of red wine, 6 bottles of Lucozade Still isotonic drink (not Red Bull), 6 cans of ginger ale. 1 good quality English language newspaper, in order of preference: *The Herald*, *The Guardian*, *The Observer*, *The New York Times*. Toaster. 1 painting by a gifted child or local amateur, 2 large, strong cardboard boxes and 4 black bin liners, 5 tickets to a local football game on the day of the show (major cities only).

MONSTER MAGNET

Coffee and hot water for 10 with condiments. 1 case of Harp beer, 1 case of Rolling Rock beer, 1 bottle each of a quality red/white wine, 1 bottle Absolut vodka, 1 bottle Jack Daniel's, 6 cases of Poland Spring water, 8 bottles of Gatorade (lemon, lime, or orange), 1 case of Coke, 1 case of Diet Coke, 1 bag of corn chips, 1 jar of salsa, 2 packs each of Marlboro Ultra Lights and Camel Filters, 2 Bic lighters, cock rings, edible panties, 1 blow-up doll (male), 1 blow-up doll (female), 1 penis enlarger, 1 helper monkey.

MÖTLEY CRÜE'S NIKKI SIXX

Whole roasted chicken; 1 vegetable tray for seven people (with proper dip); 1 deli tray for seven people; sliced whole wheat bread; 3 packets of StarKist tuna (not canned), must be chunk white; 4 bananas; 4 apples; peanut butter and strawberry jam; 2 cans of Campbell's chicken soup. 6 cans of Diet Coke, 1 case of Arrowhead water, 1 quart of skimmed milk, 4 bottles of Gatorade, 6 cans of sugar-free Red Bull. A supply of clean ice, 4 self-contained candles, 1 boa constrictor (not to be less than 15 ft), 1 machete, 1 stainless steel double-bladed combat/survival knife (not serrated), 1 fully suppressed Heckler & Koch MP-5 SD sub-machine gun and 500 9 mm rounds.

" 1 helper monkey. "

That's not average!
A FASHION THING
WIZARD OF WOR
around for longer than most of us realise
CELEBRITY SKIN
I'm a bad mutha
trouser snakes
claws in
LEATHER TROUSERS
mayhem
Other things like drugs and alcohol?
ROCK'N'METAL
squeezed
gets quite angry.
skills needed to
Campbell's
CONDENSED
Chicken Noodle
SOUP
SNAKE SNUFFING

*

THE OFFSPRING

One case of Spam, assorted bread and cheese, one large bottle of antiseptic cleaner, one large box red wine, two packs of edible undies, one gallon sulphuric acid, two and a half liters of rubbing alcohol.

ORBITAL

Large, clean, ventilated dressing room with no childish graffiti and a sea view; 40 x Topic Bars (hazelnuts removed); 2 crates Draught Guinness; mauve triple-ply toilet paper (4 rolls); 2 bottles of vodka and a packet of crisps; 4 boxes orange juice; 4 boxes cranberry juice; 20 fluffy towels (large); 4 bottles decent wine; 24 bottles of mineral water; 1 pool table; 5 Slinkies; ice; head polish. No genetically modified anything!

"5 one-hour sessions with psychologist (after show)."

✳

SUPER FURRY ANIMALS

2 Gideon Bibles, hot coffee, fresh milk, 10 boxes of Farley's Rusks, a single 50-metre roll of tin foil (preferred brand Bacofoil), a genuine message in a bottle, 10 oz of maggots, 2 fishing rods (coastal shows only), small water feature, 5 Tunisian camels, 2 bottles of quality red wine—no New World, 350 packs of King Dong condoms, any Vonda Shepard or best of Kenny G album, Faith Hill poster, 5 cigarette lighters, 1 liter of Gordon's gin, 5 one-hour sessions with psychologist (after show).

*

WESTLIFE

2 Sony Playstations, 10 games (must include 2 Tiger Woods/Gold games), 7 foot pool table, Space Invaders table, Dukes of Hazzard pinball machine with two backless stools, 2 large speakers (need tech term), entertainment deck: must include VCR, DVD multi-regional, 2 vinyl decks, 10 track CD player (minimum). 2 x 32" flat screen TVs, two acoustic guitars/Takamine, 1 two-person sofa, 1 three-person sofa, 2 arm chairs, large 6-foot deep fridge/glass door only. Breakfast: organic muesli, fresh fruit, toast/wholemeal, scrambled eggs/free-range, orange juice, whole milk. Dinner: steamed vegetables, grilled chicken breast/boneless, grilled steak, 12 Diet Cokes (checked every 60 minutes), 12 bottles still water, tea: tea bags only, 6 liter low-fat yogurt, 12 x 1 liter ice bags. Dog/band's own Labrador, shot glasses, chess set, 2 inflatable sumo outfits.

"Dog/band's own Labrador, shot glasses, chess set, 2 inflatable sumo outfits."

> "Dressing room walls covered in previous bands' graffiti and drawings of penises (minimum 4), full-color assortment of permanent markers for, oh, no reason."

✳

YO LA TENGO

Variety of ketchup, America's condiment; whole pineapple for guitar tech. UK only: fully operational Corby trouser press; second Corby trouser press, for dismantling; assortment of fresh fruit; assortment of juices; sodas for accidentally spilling on the floor (12); disgruntled house monitor engineer; espresso machine with Descendents-grade espresso beans. Dressing room walls covered in previous bands' graffiti and drawings of penises (minimum 4), full-color assortment of permanent markers for, oh, no reason.

Sue's Thanks:

A standing ovation goes to *Q* magazine for granting permissions to use the band riders featured from 1998 to 2008 and to all of the bands for giving us such fantastic material to work with, especially the weird ones!

A huge round of applause to Nigel Osbourne, John Cerullo, Bernadette Malavarca, and Hal Leonard Performing Arts Publishing Group.

My schön boy Wilf, your illustrations brought the book to life.

My drama queen Katy—love you big much. X.

Thank you to my loving and big-hearted parents David and Jeanette for their unconditional support, belief, and encouragement and my siblings, even though they haven't got a clue what I do.

The inner circle, you know who you are, and specifically Subo for true friendship and countless bars of Green & Blacks chocolate.

The Potting Shed team and Rachel for tea, tears, and triumphs—nobody does it better!

My dear friends Double D and Gary T, always putting the world to rights and helping others. You are the best.

My wonderful BFF Stella—we've gone through hell and high water together and we're still smiling.

To PR, please accept my humblest apologies that a certain Mr. Todd Rundgren is not featured!

The author Rhonda Byrne for teaching me the power of positive thinking; it rocks.

In precious memory of my dear friend and creative angel Debbie Lishman—your joyful spirit, love, and kindness will remain in my heart forever.

Wilf's Thanks:

A big thanks to all the amazing musicians whose quirky desires have furnished me with the outrageous material to work with.

Thank you to my wonderful and inspirational Mum for providing as much love, faith, support, and belief in this project as you do in my life. For her creative genes and for teaching me never to settle for lukewarm tea. Love you millions. X.

Thanks to my Dad, the coolest bloke I know, for his creative genes, encouragement, and for imparting his repertoire of good and bad jokes. Time spent down the pub putting the world to rights. For our roller-coaster days and nights and teaching me the gift of the gab—you're my best mate! Love you man. X.

To my talented younger brother and sisters, my loving Grandma and grandparents, and the rest of my wonderful and wacky family.

To all those at Bath College, Lincoln University, and Blast Radius for all of their creative advice and encouragement that was integral in developing my style. I salute you.

Hats off to all those mates and acquaintances who opened my eyes to so many things, especially true friendship, during my maturing process. You know who you are!